The Children's Litt

MW01139867

TJ Burdick
Drawings by Carly Lobenhofer & Rumi Das

This book belongs to:

_____

Nihil Obstat: Rev. Timothy Hall
                   Censor Deputatis
                   August 24, 2016

Imprimatur: † Most Rev. John Quinn
                   Bishop of Winona
                   August 24, 2016

The *imprimatur* is an official declaration that a book or pamphlet is free of doctrinal or moral error. No implication is contained therein that those who have granted the *imprimatur* agree with the contents, opinions, or statements expressed.

Scripture quotations are from New Revised Standard Version Bible: Catholic Edition, copyright © 1989, 1993 National Council of the Churches of Christ in the United States of America. Used by permission. All rights reserved.

Development editing: Jerry and Susan Windley-Daoust

Artwork: Carly Lobenhofer (pages 7, 9, 11, 13, 15, 17, 21, 23, 27, 29, 31, 35, 37, 39, 47, 55); Rumi Das (pages 19, 41, 53, 57, 59, 61); Adobe Stock (cover image, 25, 33, 45, 49, 51).

The art on page 5 is in the public domain.

Copyright © 2019, 2016 by TJ Burdick. All rights reserved. No part of this book may be reproduced by any means without the written permission of the publisher.
Printed in the United States of America

24 23 22 21 20 19   2 3 4 5 6 7 8 9

ISBN: 978-1-68192-517-2 (Inventory No. T2406)
LCCN: 2019939974

Our Sunday Visitor, Inc.
200 Noll Plaza
Huntington, IN 46750
www.osv.com

The Children's Little Advent Book

Daily Reflections and Coloring Pages for Children Ages 4–7

TJ Burdick

Drawings by Carly Lobenhofer & Rumi Das

Advent: A Journey to Jesus

I love Christmas. I know you do, too.

I also love Jesus, and I hope that you do, too.

This book joins these two loves together. It was made especially for young children (like you!) to use with your parents.

Together with your family, you will journey through Advent with Joseph, Mary, and of course, Jesus.

What is Advent, you ask? Advent is the time before Christmas when we wait for Jesus, the Son of God, to come into the world. While we wait, we read stories about how God's people, the Israelites, waited many years for a savior.

That savior was Jesus. By being born into the world, God chose to be with us in a new way. He taught us what we must do to be with him always. And he died for us on the cross so that someday, we can be with him in heaven.

Here are some things you'll need during your journey through Advent:

- 5-10 minutes of family prayer time a day
- A Bible
- Coloring crayons or pencils
- An Advent wreath and candles

Every day during Advent, you and your family will read a little bit from the Bible, talk a little bit about how to be close to Jesus, and pray together. Then you can keep on praying and thinking as you color the picture for the day.

Are you ready? Let's begin our journey through Advent!

Some Notes for Parents

- Advent is a season that can have up to twenty-six days, depending on the liturgical year. We have included twenty-eight reflections, including one for Christmas Eve and one for Christmas Day, to do with your child.

- To use this book, begin by reading the first entry on the First Sunday of Advent, and read an entry every day of Advent. If Advent is shorter than twenty-six days, skip to the entries for Christmas Eve and Christmas Day at the end of this book.

- Note that the First Sunday of Advent always falls between November 27 and December 3. It is the Sunday after the Feast of Christ the King.

- You may wish to light an Advent wreath during your daily reading from this book.

- For more ideas about what to do with your children during Advent, see the Peanut Butter & Grace website at pbgrace.com/advent.

Raphael, *Holy Family with a Palm Tree* (1506)

Day 1: Light in the Darkness

Scripture

In him was life, and the life was the light of all people. The light shines in the darkness, and the darkness did not overcome it.

—John 1:4-5

Reflection

Lighting candles is a wonderful way to begin prayer. During Advent, we light candles on our Advent wreaths to remind us that Jesus is the light of the world. The smoke that goes up from the flame represents our prayers going up to heaven. Even the heat that comes from the candle reminds us of the warmth that we feel when we know the love of God, and the love of family and friends.

• *Where do you see candles?*

Prayer

Jesus, your love is an all-encompassing flame. May we burn with that same love so that others will feel the warmth of your presence. Amen.

This is an Advent wreath. Color three candles purple, and one rose.

Day 2: Praying Alone

Scripture

But when you pray, go into your room, close the door and pray to your Father, who is unseen. Then your Father, who sees what is done in secret, will reward you."

   —*Matthew 6:6*

Reflection

The way we talk to one another is different depending on where we are and who we are with. In church, we talk with God in a large group, like at a dinner table, and we try not to interrupt. Sometimes, though, we need to interrupt our day by finding a silent place to pray so that we can talk with Jesus one-on-one.

- *Where can you go when you want to talk to Jesus one-on-one?*
- *What do you talk about with Jesus when you are alone with Him?*

Prayer

Loving God, teach us to pray as we should. May your Spirit intercede for us and help us to recognize your will so that we might follow it more closely. Amen.

It's important to take extra time to pray during Advent!

Day 3: Bless the World

Scripture

In the sixth month the angel Gabriel was sent by God to a town in Galilee called Nazareth, to a virgin engaged to a man whose name was Joseph, of the house of David. The virgin's name was Mary. And he came to her and said, "Greetings, favored one! The Lord is with you." But she was much perplexed by his words and pondered what sort of greeting this might be. The angel said to her, "Do not be afraid, Mary, for you have found favor with God. And now, you will conceive in your womb and bear a son, and you will name him Jesus."

—Luke 1:26-31

Reflection

In today's reading, the angel Gabriel told Mary that the Lord had chosen her to bless the whole world by becoming the mother of Jesus. God wants us to bless the world by sharing Jesus with it, too, just like Mary did!

• *What can you do during Advent and Christmas to bless the world?*

Prayer

Jesus Christ, make us your messengers. Give us the knowledge, wisdom and virtue to declare your glory to the ends of the earth. Amen.

How will you share Jesus with the whole world like Mary did?

Day 4: "Let It Be"

Scripture

The angel said to her, "The Holy Spirit will come upon you, and the power of the Most High will overshadow you; therefore the child to be born will be holy; he will be called Son of God. And now, your relative Elizabeth in her old age has also conceived a son; and this is the sixth month for her who was said to be barren. For nothing will be impossible with God." Then Mary said, "Here am I, the servant of the Lord; let it be with me according to your word." Then the angel departed from her.

—Luke 1:35-38

Reflection

Let it be done with me according to your word." That was the way Mary said "yes" to God's plan.

Mary may have been uncertain about whether she was ready to do what God asked of her. But she trusted God when she said: "Let it be."

- *When is it good to say "yes"? When is it good to say "no"?*
- *Why is it so good that Mary said "yes" to becoming the Mother of Jesus?*

Prayer

Holy Father, keep us close to you so that, recognizing you in our thoughts and actions, all that we are may say "yes" to you. Amen.

Mary said "yes" to God's plan!

Day 5: Joseph Learns to Trust

Scripture

An angel of the Lord appeared to him in a dream and said, "Joseph, son of David, do not be afraid to take Mary as your wife, for the child conceived in her is from the Holy Spirit."

—*Matthew 1:18-20*

Reflection

Joseph and Mary had planned to get married. But then Joseph found out Mary was going to have a baby. How could she have a baby before they were married? Joseph thought maybe they should not be married. But then God told him not to be afraid to take Mary as his wife, because it was God's plan for her to have a baby by the power of the Holy Spirit. Once he knew God's plan, Joseph said "yes" to God and married her.

God wants us to trust him when life is difficult or the way is unclear, just like Joseph did.

- *What makes you afraid?*
- *How can you trust God when you are afraid?*

Prayer

Jesus, sometimes we get confused and afraid. When those times come, help us to trust you so that we can be strong and courageous. Amen.

Joseph trusted in God's plan.

Day 6: To Love Like God

Scripture

Love is patient; love is kind; love is not envious or boastful or arrogant or rude. It does not insist on its own way; it is not irritable or resentful; it does not rejoice in wrongdoing, but rejoices in the truth. It bears all things, believes all things, hopes all things, endures all things.

Love never ends. . . .

—*1 Corinthians 13:4-8*

Reflection

The Christmas spirit is in us! Family is close and we are getting closer to celebrating the birth of Jesus. Let's not forget the reason for the season: God loves us, and so we should love one another in the same way. Jesus loved us so much, he gave his whole heart to us!

- *What did Jesus do for us because he loves us?*
- *What did you do today to love someone?*

Prayer

Baby Jesus, you came to save us from our sins. May our every action give you glory! May we give thanks for the sacrifice you made by sacrificing for others. Amen.

The Sacred Heart of Jesus is a symbol of how much Jesus loves us!

Day 7: Good News!

Scripture

In those days Mary set out and went with haste to a Judean town in the hill country, where she entered the house of Zechariah and greeted Elizabeth. When Elizabeth heard Mary's greeting, the child leaped in her womb. And Elizabeth was filled with the Holy Spirit and exclaimed with a loud cry, "Blessed are you among women, and blessed is the fruit of your womb. And why has this happened to me, that the mother of my Lord comes to me? For as soon as I heard the sound of your greeting, the child in my womb leaped for joy. And blessed is she who believed that there would be a fulfillment of what was spoken to her by the Lord."

Luke 1: 39–45

Reflection

Everyone wants to share good news! In today's reading, Mary travels to tell Elizabeth the good news that Jesus, the Son of God, is coming.

- *What good news can you share with your family today?*

Prayer

Heavenly Father, you sent your son to us, and Mary could not help spreading the good news! Help us to share the good news about Jesus with everyone we meet. Amen.

What is Mary saying to Elizabeth? What is Elizabeth saying to Mary?

Day 8: The First Christmas Carol

Scripture

And Mary said, "My soul magnifies the Lord, and my spirit rejoices in God my Savior, for he has looked with favor on the lowliness of his servant. Surely, from now on all generations will call me blessed."

   —Luke 1:46-48

Reflection

Christmas has a joyful sound to it. The silence of winter, the crackling of a fire and of course, the beautiful songs that we sing together. Mary was so excited to become Jesus' mother that she started the first Christmas carol when she started singing God's praises!

- *What was Mary's song about?*
- *Why do you think she sang it?*
- *What is your favorite Christmas carol?*

Prayer

Holy Spirit, you strum within our souls the rhythm and rhyme of true joy. May our hearts and minds overflow with praise to the God who created us, forever and ever. Amen.

We welcome Jesus with beautiful music and singing!

Day 9: Fear God? Why?

Scripture

His mercy is for those who fear him from generation to generation. He has shown strength with his arm; he has scattered the proud in the thoughts of their hearts. He has brought down the powerful from their thrones, and lifted up the lowly."

—*Luke 1: 50-52*

Reflection

In her song, Mary sang that God shows mercy to those who fear him. But if God is love, why should we fear him? Well, there are two ways we can be afraid of God: We can fear that he will punish us for our sins, or we can fear doing and saying things that make him sad.

- *Which one of those fears shows the most love?*
- *What type of fear do you think Mary sang about in her song?*
- *Do you think God wants you to be afraid of Him?*

Prayer

God, at times we fear too much. Other times, we fear too little. Help our fears to be united to your love so that we may be comforted and encouraged to do what you want us to do. Amen.

If you are ever afraid, pray to God!

Day 10: Home for Christmas

Scripture

And Mary remained with [Elizabeth] about three months and then returned to her home.

— *Luke 1: 56*

Reflection

Family is one of the greatest gifts Jesus gives to us. Christmas is a perfect time for family to come together and share their love for one another, just as Mary returned to her home and family. Together, Mary, Joseph, and Jesus would make a new family . . . the Holy Family!

- *Who will you celebrate Christmas with this year?*
- *Will you celebrate Christmas at home, or will you visit someone?*
- *What are some reasons you love the people in your family?*

Prayer

Blessed Trinity, you sent your Son to become part of a family. Bless our own families so that we can be more holy. Teach us patience, wisdom, and humility. Amen.

Draw a picture of your family.

Day 11: We're on a Mission

Scripture

And you, child, will be called the prophet of the Most High; for you will go before the Lord to prepare his ways, to give knowledge of salvation to his people by the forgiveness of their sins."

—*Luke 1:76-77*

Reflection

In today's reading, the prophet Simeon announces the mission of Jesus. A mission is something you do to make the world a better place. The mission of every Christian is to love God and others just as Jesus did. God calls each of us to a special mission, too—one that only you can complete! What is your mission? You can find out by praying on your own and in Church, and listening to what God says in the Bible and your heart. Your parents will help you discover your mission, too.

- *What was Jesus' mission?*
- *What are some of the missions God calls you to do at home? At school?*

Prayer

Holy Father, we know you have something very special for us to do. Please light up our hearts and minds and bless us with the talents necessary to complete the mission you give us. Amen.

God helps us complete our mission with a superpower called "grace"!

Day 12: Because We Love

Scripture

For a child has been born for us, a son given to us; authority rests upon his shoulders; and he is named Wonderful Counselor, Mighty God, Everlasting Father, Prince of Peace.

— Isaiah 9:6

Reflection

A lot of children believe that if they are good before Christmas, they will receive many presents. But that's not the best reason to be good. We should be good because we love others, even when it gets difficult to love them. When we are good, we bring peace to our home and our family. Jesus, who is the Prince of Peace, can help us be good, if we ask him.

- *What does the word* peace *mean?*
- *What happens if you misbehave at home?*
- *Who can you ask for help if you are having trouble being good?*

Prayer

Jesus, we are right to call you the Prince of Peace. Help us to always desire peace so that one day, we will experience your peace forever. Amen.

A dove carrying an olive branch is a symbol of peace.

Day 13: The Father of Lights

Scripture

Every generous act of giving, with every perfect gift, is from above, coming down from the Father of lights, with whom there is no variation or shadow due to change.

— *James 1: 17*

Reflection

Do you know anyone who is afraid of the dark? Do you know anyone who is afraid of light? Everyone prefers light to darkness, which is why God the Father is known as "the Father of Lights" and Jesus is known as "the Light of the World." As we light our candles on the Advent wreath today, remember that even though we blow them out, God's light can always remain in our hearts.

- *Why do we light candles on our Advent wreath?*
- *Who can help you if you are afraid of the dark?*

Prayer

Father, we thank you for your light in our lives. May we reflect your heavenly light in the world so that everyone who sees us will see your love. Amen.

Every time you do something loving, you let God's light shine.

Day 14: Welcoming the King

Scripture

Herod inquired of [the scribes] where the Messiah was to be born. They told him, "In Bethlehem of Judea. . . ." Then Herod secretly called for the wise men and learned from them the exact time when the star had appeared. Then he sent them to Bethlehem, saying, "Go and search diligently for the child; and when you have found him, bring me word so that I may also go and pay him homage."

    — *Matthew 2:4-8*

Reflection

King Herod heard that the Messiah was going to be born in the town of Bethlehem. The Messiah would be the savior of Israel, and more powerful than any king. King Herod was jealous, so he sent the wise men to find the newborn Messiah. He said that he wanted to honor the Messiah, but really, he wanted to get rid of him.

- *Do you know who the Messiah was?*
- *King Herod wanted to hurt the baby Jesus. How do we hurt Jesus?*

Prayer

Christ Child, we adore you, but we also hurt you when we sin. Help us to never desire to do wrong on purpose, but enlighten us with your truth so that we can follow it more perfectly. Amen.

Sometimes we call Jesus "king" because he rules heaven and earth.

Day 15: Every Nation

Scripture

When they had heard the king, they set out; and there, ahead of them went the star that they had seen at its rising, until it stopped over the place where the child was.

— *Matthew 2:9*

Reflection

The three kings, also known as the three wise men, came from a far-off land to see Jesus. They were so interested in seeing him that they left their homes, families, and friends to travel across a dangerous desert. They knew that they didn't want to miss the first Christmas!

Christmas is celebrated wherever there are Christians. In the United States we celebrate the birth of Jesus with lights, candy canes, presents and, of course, our loved ones.

- *What is your family's favorite Christmas tradition?*
- *What far-off land would you like to visit? How do you think they celebrate Christmas there?*

Prayer

Father God, we celebrate your love for all the people of the world. Thank you for sending your Son to be a light to the whole world. Give us the grace we need to bring your light to the people of every nation. Amen.

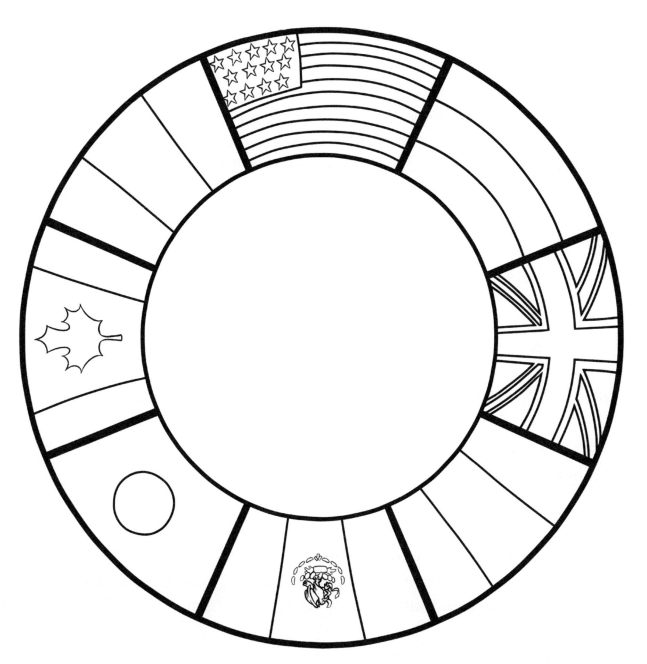

Ask your parents for help coloring these flags from around the world.

Day 16: Rules

Scripture

In those days a decree went out from Emperor Augustus that all the world should be registered. . . . All went to their own towns to be registered. Joseph also went from the town of Nazareth in Galilee to Judea, to the city of David called Bethlehem, because he was descended from the house and family of David. He went to be registered with Mary, to whom he was engaged and who was expecting a child.

— *Luke 2:1-5*

Reflection

When the emperor made a rule that everyone had to be registered, or counted, Joseph and Mary had to travel to Bethlehem, because that is where Joseph's family was from. That's why Jesus was born in Bethlehem, not Nazareth—all because of a rule about counting!

- *Why do we have rules at home and in school?*
- *What kinds of rules are easy to follow? Which ones are hardest?*

Prayer

Jesus, you traveled in your mother's womb to be counted among earthly men and women. May we be counted among those who dwell in heaven one day. On that day, may we sing in eternal joy with you. Amen.

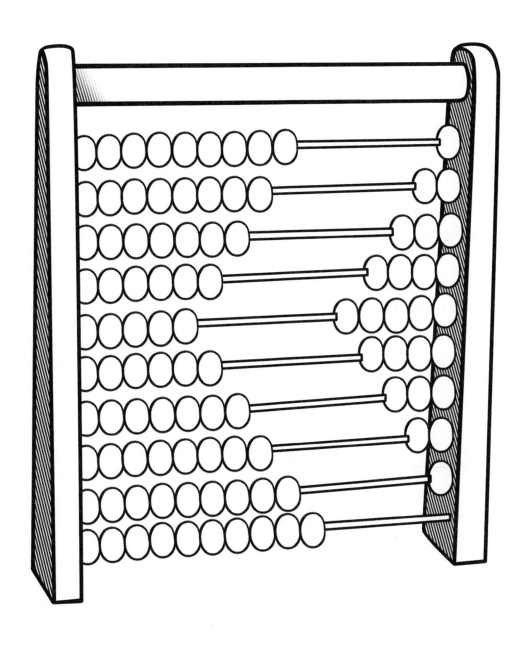

This is an abacus, which ancient people used for counting.

Day 17: No Room in the Inn

Scripture

There was no place for them in the inn.
— *Luke 2:7*

Reflection

Mary and Joseph had quite the task of protecting Jesus. They had to travel many miles to get to their destination of Bethlehem. When they finally arrived, there was no room in the inn. No one would give the King of the Universe a place to stay! This is the way God chose to be with us, living as a human being in a crowded, sometimes unwelcoming world.

- *How could you welcome Jesus into your life today?*
- *Jesus came down to be more like us. What could you do today to be more like Him?*

Prayer

Blessed Son of the Father, Jesus, there was no room for you in the inn. May we be made worthy to have you enter under our roofs. Help us open our hearts to allow you in. Amen.

People shut their doors when the baby Jesus needed a place to stay.

Day 18: Angels!

Scripture

When Herod died, an angel of the Lord suddenly appeared in a dream to Joseph in Egypt and said, "Get up, take the child and his mother, and go to the land of Israel, for those who were seeking the child's life are dead." Then Joseph got up, took the child and his mother, and went to the land of Israel.

— *Matthew 2:19-21*

Reflection

Angels are God's messengers. In today's reading, an angel sends Joseph the message that it is safe to come back home to Nazareth because King Herod could no longer harm Jesus.

The Church tells us that each one of us has a personal angel that protects us and prays with us. This angel is known as our guardian angel. Most of the time, we cannot see angels, because they do not have bodies. But we can pray to them and ask them to help us to do what is good.

- *Do you pray to your guardian angel?*

Prayer

God, thank you for the blessing of our guardian angels. May we enjoy their friendship so that we might hear you more clearly. Amen.

Angels lead us to God.

Day 19: Waiting...

Scripture

But when the fullness of time had come, God sent his Son, born of a woman, born under the law, in order to redeem those who were under the law, so that we might receive adoption as children.

— *Galatians 4:4-5*

Reflection

Time is a wonderful thing, but it can make us very tired when we are kept waiting. Sometimes we wait in line for our turn on the swing or we wait until dinner is served with grumbling tummies. We know that when the time comes, we will be happy, but it is still hard to wait.

It took God a long time to prepare the world for Christmas! If you are tired from waiting, rest peacefully tonight. Christmas is almost here.

• *Tell us about a time you had to wait for something. Was it worth the wait?*

Prayer

God, give us the gift of patience. Provide us with the grace to wait for your Word to enter into our hearts more fully. Amen.

December

1 2 3 4 5
6 7 8 9 10
11 12 13 14 15
16 17 18 19 20
21 22 23 24 25

How many days until Christmas? Color all the days that have passed.

Day 20: Are You Ready?

Scripture

Then he told them a parable: "Look at the fig tree and all the trees; as soon as they sprout leaves you can see for yourselves and know that summer is already near. So also, when you see these things taking place, you know that the kingdom of God is near."

    —*Luke 21:28-31*

Reflection

Christmas spirit is all around us. The decorations, parties, Church activities and preparations are all upon us. What is more important, though, is the feeling of love that surrounds our Christmas cheer. This love makes us happy, excited and, most of all, thoughtful of others. That is what the Christmas spirit is all about!

- *How many more days are there until Christmas?*
- *Have you gotten everything ready?*
- *Can you get something ready for Jesus?*

Prayer

God, make our hearts ready to receive your Son not only today, but every day. Amen.

The Christmas tree reminds us that Jesus is coming soon.

Day 21: A Birthday for Jesus

Scripture

The people who walked in darkness have seen a great light; those who lived in a land of deep darkness— on them light has shined.

— Isaiah 9:2

Reflection

Nobody knows the actual day when Jesus was born, but we celebrate his birth on Christmas day, December 25th. This is about the time of year when the sun begins to shine on the northern part of the Earth for more and more time. The return of the sun reminds us that Jesus is also the "great light" who brings us out of the darkness of sin.

- *When is your birthday?*
- *Why is sunlight so important for the earth?*
- *Why is Jesus so important to the world?*

Prayer

Jesus, even in very long nights, your saving light shines. Shine your light in us, especially during our darkest moments, so that we may see ourselves as your sons and daughters. Amen.

The sun reminds us that Jesus gives us light and life.

Day 22: Needing and Wanting

Scripture

When they saw that the star had stopped, they were overwhelmed with joy. On entering the house, they saw the child with Mary his mother; and they knelt down and paid him homage. Then, opening their treasure chests, they offered him gifts of gold, frankincense, and myrrh.

— *Matthew 2:10-11*

Reflection

Presents are a lot of fun to give and receive during Christmas. There are two types of gifts that people give: gifts that people want and gifts that people need. Jesus is a gift from God that we all need. We should be most thankful for the gifts that we need, especially the gift of Jesus!

- *What is the difference between needing and wanting something?*
- *What is a gift you needed? What is a gift you wanted?*
- *What gifts does Jesus want from us on his birthday?*

Prayer

Christ, you are the gift that all people need. May we receive you into our hearts and give your love to others every day of our lives. Amen.

What gifts wil you give Jesus? Draw a picture of them in the boxes.

Day 23: Sacrificing

Scripture

For God so loved the world that he gave his only Son, so that everyone who believes in him may not perish but may have eternal life.

— John 3:16

Reflection

In Jesus, God gave all of himself to us. Another way of saying this is that he sacrificed himself for us. Do you know what a sacrifice is? It is giving up something important or valuable for the sake of something better.

Christmas is a time for giving. Let's make a sacrifice of our own so that we can better understand the Father's love for us.

- *What can you sacrifice today to help you think about God's love for us more often?*

Prayer

Father, you taught us the meaning of sacrifice when you sacrificed your only Son so that we might be saved. May we become more like you, rich in sacrifice for the salvation of souls. Amen.

Jesus gave his whole self to us on the cross. What will you give to Jesus?

Day 24: How to Become Wise

Scripture

And having been warned in a dream not to return to Herod, they left for their own country by another road.

— *Matthew 2:12*

Reflection

To be wise means to understand things that really matter. The three wise men found out what matters! In their journey to Jesus, they learned:

1. That to see him, they would need to cross a long desert.
2. That giving was better than receiving.
3. That after meeting Jesus, they cannot return home the same way.

You can tell who the people are who really know Jesus because of their love. After meeting him, they know no other way to act unless it is out of love. In fact, when no one who goes to meet Jesus returns as the same person; instead, they find their true self in him.

- *Who is a wise person you know? How is that person wise?*

Prayer

Jesus, be our guiding light on the journey to you. Help us to act more like you. May our every action have its source in your love. Amen.

The wise men followed the light of the star of Bethlehem to find Jesus.

Day 25: God Fills the Silence

Scripture

In that region there were shepherds living in the fields, keeping watch over their flock by night. Then an angel of the Lord stood before them, and the glory of the Lord shone around them, and they were terrified. But the angel said to them, "Do not be afraid; for see—I am bringing you good news of great joy for all the people: to you is born this day in the city of David a Savior, who is the Messiah, the Lord. . . ." And suddenly there was with the angel a multitude of the heavenly host, praising God and saying, "Glory to God in the highest heaven, and on earth peace among those whom he favors!"

— *Luke 2:8-14*

Reflection

The shepherds were probably enjoying the silence of the night. But then that silence was filled with the joyful sound of angels singing! Let's take time to be silent today, so God might fill the silence with joy.

- *What sounds do you hear during Christmas?*
- *How long can you be silent? Try it! Listen for angels in the silence.*

Prayer

Holy Spirit, in the silence of our hearts you speak to us. Help us to clear away the noise so that we can hear you better, and receive your gifts of peace and joy. Amen.

"Do not be afraid," the angel said, "for I bring you good news."

Day 26 • Christmas Joy

Scripture

When the angels had left them and gone into heaven, the shepherds said to one another, "Let us go now to Bethlehem and see this thing that has taken place, which the Lord has made known to us." So they went with haste and found Mary and Joseph, and the child lying in the manger. . . .

The shepherds returned, glorifying and praising God for all they had heard and seen, as it had been told them.

— *Luke 2:15-16, 20*

Reflection

The shepherds were changed after meeting Jesus. Before, they enjoyed the silence of their work, but upon their return they couldn't keep from singing—just like Mary and Elizabeth sang. Everyone who learned that the Messiah was coming in Jesus responded with joy. That's why we sing joyful songs every Christmas!

- *What is the most joyful Christmas song you know?*
- *What do you like most about it?*

Prayer

Holy Father, may a song of praise forever be on our lips and the joy of your salvation forever be written onto our minds and hearts. May we give you the praise that is worthy of your name. Amen.

What songs are these children singing?

Christmas Eve • December 24

Scripture

While they were there, the time came for her to deliver her child. And she gave birth to her firstborn son and wrapped him in bands of cloth, and laid him in a manger. . . .

— *Luke 2:6-7*

Reflection

The time has come. The night is silent and the Christmas spirit is all around us. Today is the darkest day of the year, the day when we receive the least amount of light from the sun. Can you imagine how dark it must have been in the stable the night before Jesus was born? Tonight, notice the darkness of the night. Tomorrow, we receive the Light of the World!

- *How do you think it felt to be in the darkness of the stable the night before Christ was born?*

Prayer

Mother of God Incarnate, tonight we wait together patiently for the coming of our Lord Jesus Christ. May the joy we experience upon his arrival into our hearts lay the foundation for our eternal life with him and you in heaven. Amen.

The animals made room for Jesus. How have you made room for him?

Christmas • December 25

Scripture

And all who heard it were amazed at what the shepherds told them. But Mary treasured all these words and pondered them in her heart.

—Luke 2:18-19

Reflection

What did Mary do on the day that Jesus was born? She treasured everything that had happened, and pondered them in her heart. To "ponder" is to think about something very carefully, to turn it over and look at it from different angles so that we can understand its meaning.

On this Christmas Day, take time to "treasure and ponder" the true meaning of the birth of Jesus.

One last thing: Be sure to say "thank you" to Jesus for being born.

• *Say a prayer to Jesus in your own words.*

Prayer

O God, we worship you in your Son, Jesus, the Word made flesh. Grant that we may share in the divinity of Christ, who humbled himself to share in our humanity. We ask this through his holy name. Amen.

Thank you, Jesus, for coming to be with us!